WHAT'S SPACE TOURISM?

By Jennifer Lombardo

Published in 2024 by
KidHaven Publishing, an Imprint of Greenhaven Publishing, LLC
2544 Clinton Street
Buffalo, NY 14224

Designer: Deanna Paternostro
Editor: Jennifer Lombardo

Photo credits: Cover (top), p. 5 Dima Zel/Shutterstock.com; cover (bottom) Rido/Shutterstock.com; p. 7 24K-Production/Shutterstock.com; p. 9 IrinaK/Shutterstock.com; p. 11 (Earth) peipeiro/Shutterstock.com; p. 11 (rockets) IhorZigor/Shutterstock.com; p. 13 aappp/Shutterstock.com; p. 15 Astronaut Scott Kelly/NASA; p. 17 Richard Whitcombe/Shutterstock.com; p. 19 Olena Gaidarzhy/Shutterstock.com; p. 21 Valery Brozhinsky/Shutterstock.com.

Cataloging-in-Publication Data

Names: Lombardo, Jennifer.
Title: What's space tourism? / Jennifer Lombardo.
Description: Buffalo, New York : KidHaven Publishing, 2024. | Series: What's the issue?| Includes glossary and index.
Identifiers: ISBN 9781534544147 (pbk.) | ISBN 9781534544154 (library bound) | ISBN 9781534544161 (ebook)
Subjects: LCSH: Space tourism–Juvenile literature. | Manned space flight–Juvenile literature. | Space industrialization–Juvenile literature.
Classification: LCC TL793.L686 2024 | DDC 910.919–dc23

Printed in the United States of America

Some of the images in this book illustrate individuals who are models. The depictions do not imply actual situations or events.

CPSIA compliance information: Batch #CSKH24: For further information contact Greenhaven Publishing LLC at 1-844-317-7404.

Please visit our website, www.greenhavenpublishing.com. For a free color catalog of all our high-quality books, call toll free 1-844-317-7404 or fax 1-844-317-7405.

Find us on

CONTENTS

The First Astronauts

In 1961, people went to outer space for the first time in history. The first human to do this was a Russian man named Yuri Gagarin. He flew to space in April of that year. One month later, Alan Shepard became the first American to go to space.

Since then, there have been many other astronauts from countries all over the world. They do science experiments on the International Space Station (ISS). Learning about what happens to living things in space helps us understand more about them on Earth.

Facing the Facts

The first living creature to make an orbital flight, or a flight around Earth, was a dog named Laika. The Russians sent her to space in 1957. Sadly, she didn't live long because the Russians hadn't made a plan to bring her back to Earth.

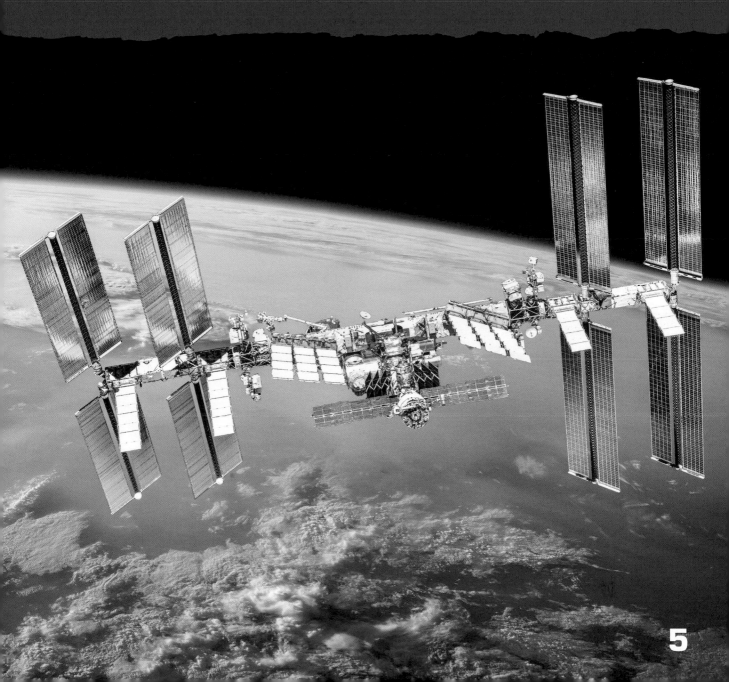

Astronauts live and work on the ISS (shown here).

Tourists in Space

Many people like to travel. People who travel to another place for fun are called tourists. Earth is big, and there are a lot of places on it to **explore**. However, many people want to go even farther—to space!

There are many reasons why people want to visit space. One is that they want to feel what it's like not to be weighed down by **gravity**. Another is that they want to see the stars and planets all around them. Some people just want to try something very few people have ever done!

Facing the Facts 🔍

In 2010, an author named Frank Cottrell Boyce wrote a book called *Cosmic* that imagined what being a space tourist would be like.

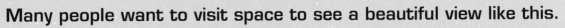
Many people want to visit space to see a beautiful view like this.

The Big Three

Space tourism hasn't taken off yet, but it isn't exactly new. People have been visiting space for fun since 2001. However, their choices were very limited. They could only leave Earth from Russia, and they had to stay at the ISS.

Today, three companies are leading the way in space tourism. They want to make it easier for everyone to take a trip to space without getting in the way of the astronauts working on the ISS. These companies are Blue Origin, SpaceX, and Virgin Galactic. Other companies working on space tourism are Boeing, Axiom Space, and Space Perspective.

Facing the Facts

Dennis Tito was the world's first space tourist. He visited the ISS for 1 week in 2001. The trip, which he booked through a company called Space Adventures, cost him $20 million.

Shown here is an early **version** of SpaceX's spacecraft.

Orbital or Suborbital?

The two kinds of spaceflights are orbital and suborbital. The difference between the two is the **trajectory** of the flight. The speed of the spacecraft decides its trajectory. If the spacecraft is moving slower than 17,500 miles (28,000 km) per hour, it will fall back to Earth at some point. If it moves faster than that, it will stay in space, circling the planet, until it's ready to reenter the **atmosphere**.

As of 2022, Virgin Galactic and Blue Origin are working on suborbital flights. A suborbital flight can last anywhere from a few minutes to a few days, but most companies are offering only very short trips. For example, a suborbital flight with Blue Origin lasts 11 minutes. Axiom and Boeing are working on orbital flights. SpaceX wants to send tourists to the moon one day.

Facing the Facts

Some people think a suborbital flight doesn't reach space, but that isn't true! It just means it comes back down on its own at some point.

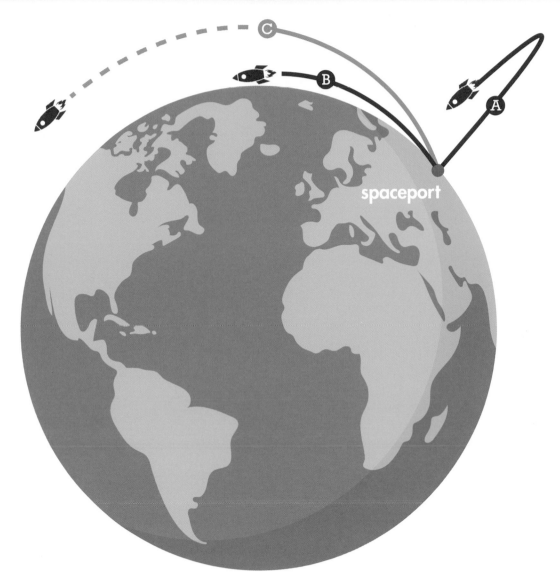

(A): short suborbital flight

(B): long suborbital flight

(C): orbital flight

The angle at which a flight is **launched** also affects its time in space. A suborbital flight won't stay in space long enough to make a full orbit around Earth. An orbital flight will.

Getting Ready

Not everyone will be able to be a space tourist, especially for an orbital trip. Just like a hiker climbing Mount Everest (the world's tallest mountain on land), a space tourist has to be **physically** fit. They also have to take a training course. Astronauts train for hundreds of hours, but a tourist only has to train for a few days.

Space tourism training covers things such as what to do on launch and reentry, as well as how to do normal things in zero gravity. This includes how to go to the bathroom! Without gravity, waste can float away from the toilet if a person isn't careful.

Facing the Facts

Going to space as a tourist doesn't make a person an astronaut. Real astronauts have to go to college and train for flight. It takes about 10 years to become an astronaut.

Training the body helps prepare it for the g-forces people **experience** during launch and reentry. G-forces create a feeling of weight caused by acceleration, or speeding up. It's the same feeling people get on a roller coaster loop, but the feeling is stronger on a spacecraft.

Barriers to Space Travel

Space travel will get cheaper as it becomes more common, but it might never be cheap enough for everyone to afford. As of 2022, a ticket can cost more than $100,000. Suborbital flights are cheaper because they're shorter than orbital flights.

In the future, booking a spaceflight might be as easy as buying a plane ticket. However, as of 2022, companies are taking **applications** for their flights. They get to pick who's allowed to go. There aren't many seats on the spacecraft, so even if people have the money, they might have to wait months or years for their turn.

Facing the Facts

Space Perspective is working on a balloon filled with hydrogen gas that will float up into space and back down again. The trip would take about 6 hours total and cost $125,000 per person.

Astronaut Scott Kelly took this photo from the ISS. Many people are willing to pay a lot of money to see the same view. Astronauts have said that seeing it in person is even better than seeing photos.

Should We Go?

Some people think going to space is a bad idea. A big reason for this is that getting the companies up and running costs billions of dollars. Many people believe that money would be better spent on Earth. There are a lot of people who need homes, food, clean water, and other important things.

Some people also think we should explore all of Earth before we move on to space. Many parts of the ocean and the rain forests haven't been explored. These places could hold important scientific discoveries.

Facing the Facts

Space travel can be very dangerous, or unsafe, even for trained astronauts. Some people worry that space tourism companies will care more about making money than about making sure their customers are safe.

Many medicines that people use every day have come from plants found in rain forests. Some people think we could find other important things in parts of the world we haven't explored yet.

Other Experiences

Not everyone will be able to go to space—especially while the tourism companies are still working on their flights. However, there are experiences people can have here on Earth that are similar, or almost the same.

People who want to feel what zero gravity is like can book a plane flight that travels in the same trajectory as a suborbital flight. It doesn't go as high or as fast, but travelers will still feel a few moments of weightlessness. Scuba diving can also make people feel weightless. Being underwater isn't exactly the same as being in space, but the way people move around is similar.

Facing the Facts

A company called Orbital Assembly Corporation is working on the first space hotels. The company hopes to open the first one in 2025 and the second in 2027.

Scuba divers not only get to feel like they're moving around in zero gravity, they also get to look at ocean life while they swim.

Looking to the Future

It will be a long time before the average person can take a vacation to space. However, we know that companies are going to keep moving forward with their plans because a lot of people want space tourism to become a reality. Over time, the price will likely get a lot lower.

If you want to go to space someday, it's important to learn more about it. Read about the dangers of space travel and what companies are doing to make their trips safe. You could even become an astronaut if you want to be in charge of the spacecraft!

20

Facing the Facts 🔍

In the 1940s, a plane ticket for a flight across the United States could cost more than $4,000 in today's money. Now, people can often find tickets for that same flight for under $500.

WHAT CAN YOU DO?

Learn about what being in space feels like and how it affects the human body.

Read more about the training space tourists and astronauts have to do.

Write to space tourism companies, asking them to use some of their money to help people here on Earth.

Visit a planetarium or science museum to learn about space.

If space interests you, learn more about jobs you can get in that field.

By the time you're an adult, you may be able to take a quick, inexpensive flight to space! Until then, here are some things you can do if you're interested in space travel.

GLOSSARY

application: A form used for making a request.

atmosphere: The thick layer of gases that surrounds Earth.

experience: To do something or live through something, or something one has done or lived through.

explore: To go into or travel over for purposes of discovery or adventure.

gravity: The force that pulls objects toward the center of a planet or star, including the center of Earth.

launch: To take off from the ground.

physically: Relating to the body.

trajectory: The curve that a body, such as a planet in its orbit or a rocket, travels along in space.

version: A form of something that is different from others.

FOR MORE INFORMATION

WEBSITES

Academic Kids: Space Tourism
academickids.com/encyclopedia/index.php/Space_tourism
Learn more facts about space tourism.

Easy Science for Kids: Space Travel
easyscienceforkids.com/all-about-space-travel/
Read about the history of space travel.

BOOKS

Jefferis, David. *Space Tourists*. New York, NY: Crabtree Publishing, 2018.

Kurtz, Kevin. *Cutting-Edge Space Tourism*. Minneapolis, MN: Lerner Publications, 2020.

Stone, Jerry, and Peter Bond. *Space Travel*. New York, NY: DK Publishing, 2019.

INDEX